Welcome to the Thrift Savings Plan!

The TSP offers these important features to help you save for retirement:

- You benefit from low administrative costs that help keep more money in your account.

- You have a choice of making traditional (pre-tax) and/or Roth (after-tax) contributions.

- FERS employees are eligible for agency automatic and matching contributions.

- You can invest in:

  - Lifecycle Funds, an automated investment tool which combines the TSP stock, bond, and Government securities funds in professionally determined proportions based on when you expect to need the money; or

  - Individual TSP Funds, which you can combine in any way you choose.

- You can transfer money from other eligible employer plans or traditional individual retirement accounts (IRAs) to your TSP account.

- If you are age 50 or older, you may be able to make additional catch-up contributions.

- If the need arises, you can borrow from your account.

- While still employed, you can make an in-service withdrawal for financial hardship or after age 59½.

- After you separate, you have a choice of withdrawal options. You can also leave your money in the TSP.

To get the most out of the TSP, you need to make several important decisions about your account. This booklet will help you get started.

Getting Started

Enrolling in the TSP

All newly hired (or rehired) civilian (FERS and CSRS) employees are automatically enrolled in the TSP. If you are automatically enrolled, your agency will deduct 3% from your basic pay (before taxes) every pay period and deposit it into your TSP account, unless you make an election to change or stop these contributions.[1] These contributions will be invested in the Government Securities Investment (G) Fund until you make a different contribution allocation.

To begin making TSP contributions if you are a member of the uniformed services, or if you are not a new hire and are not currently contributing, you must submit Form TSP-1, Election Form (TSP-U-1 for members of the uniformed services) to your agency or service. This form is available from your TSP representative[2] or the TSP website. Some agencies and services require electronic enrollment through systems such as Employee Express, LiteBlue, EBIS, myPay, or the NFC PPS. Check with your agency or service to see which one it requires.

To take advantage of this important retirement benefit, you should start as early as you can and consider contributing as much as you can.

---

[1] You may be able to request a refund of contributions made under the automatic enrollment program. See page 19 or visit the TSP website for more information about refunds.

[2] Your TSP representative is generally a person in your personnel or human resources office.

Types of Contributions

There are several types of contributions that can be made to your TSP account:

Employee Contributions

- *Regular Employee Contributions* are payroll deductions that come out of your basic pay either before taxes are withheld (traditional) or after taxes have been withheld (Roth). (See page 5 for more information about traditional and Roth tax treatments for your employee contributions.) Each pay period, your agency or service will deduct your contribution from your pay in the amount you choose (or 3% if you have been automatically enrolled) and send your contribution to the TSP. Your agency or service will continue to do this until you make a new TSP election to change your contribution or stop it, or until you reach the Internal Revenue Code (IRC) contribution limit (see pages 7–8).

  Note for members of the uniformed services: In addition to basic pay, you can also contribute 1 to 100 percent of any incentive pay, special pay, or bonus pay—as long as you elect to contribute from basic pay. However, your total contributions from all types of pay must not exceed the IRC annual additions (section 415 (c)) limit (see page 8).

- *Catch-Up Employee Contributions* are payroll deductions that participants who are age 50 or older may be eligible to make in addition to regular employee contributions. If you turn age 50 or older during the calendar year and expect to reach the IRC contribution limit for regular employee contributions, you can make additional traditional and/or Roth "catch-up" contributions. You must make a separate election for these contributions using Form TSP-1-C, Catch-Up Contribution Election (TSP-U-1-C for members of the uniformed services). Each pay period, your agency or service will make your contribution to the TSP from your pay in the amount you choose. Your catch-up contributions will stop automatically when you meet the IRC catch-up contribution limit (see page 8) or at the end of the calendar year, whichever comes first. Your catch-up contributions will not continue from year to year; you have to make a new election for each calendar year.

Note for members of the uniformed services: You cannot make catch-up contributions from incentive pay, special pay, or bonus pay. Also, you cannot make traditional catch-up contributions from tax-exempt pay. Only Roth catch-up contributions are allowed from tax-exempt pay.

Agency Contributions[3] (for FERS employees only)

If you are a *FERS* employee, you can receive two types of agency contributions:

* *Agency Automatic (1%) Contributions* — equal to 1% of your basic pay — are deposited into your TSP account every pay period, beginning the first time you are paid. These contributions are not taken out of your pay. Your agency gives them to you whether or not you contribute from your own pay.

* *Agency Matching Contributions* are made by agencies to the TSP accounts of FERS employees who contribute their own money to the TSP. Your agency matches your contributions dollar-for-dollar on the first 3% of basic pay you contribute per pay period, and 50 cents on the dollar on the next 2%. If you make both traditional and Roth employee contributions, the total percentage of pay you contribute will be used to calculate your Agency Matching Contributions.

Together, these agency contributions can equal as much as 5% of your basic pay. But you must contribute at least 5% in order to receive the full amount of agency money. This includes employees who were automatically enrolled. If you were automatically

---

[3] All agency contributions will be deposited into the traditional balance of your TSP account.

enrolled, your contribution rate is 3%, so you are not earning the maximum matching contributions that are possible for you. Consider increasing your contributions to at least 5% of your basic pay if you have not already done so. You do not need to complete a waiting period to be eligible to receive either type of agency contribution.

To increase the amount of your employee contributions, submit the TSP Election Form (TSP-1 for civilians, TSP-U-1 for members of the uniformed services) to your agency or service, or use your agency's or service's electronic version of the form.

Tax Treatments for Your TSP Employee Contributions

The TSP offers you two tax treatments for your employee contributions when you make a contribution election:

- *Traditional (pre-tax) Contributions* come out of your pay before taxes are calculated and are deposited into the traditional balance[4] of your TSP account. You pay Federal income taxes on these contributions and their earnings when you withdraw them.

   Note for members of the uniformed services: Contributions made from tax-exempt pay to a traditional balance are not subject to Federal income tax. However, the earnings associated with these contributions are taxable when withdrawn.

- *Roth (after-tax) Contributions* come out of your pay after taxes are calculated and are deposited into the Roth balance[5] of your TSP account.

---

[4] A traditional balance consists of any employee contributions (including tax-exempt contributions from pay earned in a combat zone) that you designate as traditional contributions when you make your contribution election, all agency contributions, and the earnings associated with these contributions.

[5] A Roth balance consists of any employee contributions (including tax-exempt contributions from pay earned in a combat zone) that you designate as Roth contributions when you make your contribution election, and the earnings associated with these contributions.

You pay no Federal income taxes on these contributions when you withdraw them. Roth earnings are tax-free when withdrawn as long as the following two conditions have been met: (1) 5 years have passed since January 1 of the calendar year in which you made your first Roth contribution, and (2) you have reached age 59½, have a permanent disability, or have died. Note: The TSP cannot certify to the IRS that you meet the Internal Revenue Code's definition of disability when your taxes are reported. Therefore, you must provide the justification to the IRS when you file your taxes.

Note for members of the uniformed services: Contributions made from tax-exempt pay to a Roth balance are treated the same as after-tax Roth contributions for tax reporting purposes. This means that you will not pay taxes on these contributions when you withdraw them. In addition, the earnings will be tax-free when withdrawn as long as you have met the conditions previously mentioned.

You can make both traditional and Roth contributions, and you can change your election at any time. If you choose to make both types of contributions, your account will be made up of two separate balances — traditional and Roth. These two balances will keep your contributions, earnings, and any money you transfer into (or out of) your TSP account separate for tax purposes, but any loans, withdrawals, contribution allocations, and interfund transfers you make will include a proportional amount from each balance. You will not be able to take out, borrow from, or change the investment of, just one balance. Also, you will not be able to convert one type of balance into another.

For more detailed information about how traditional and Roth contributions may impact your paycheck and account savings over time, see the TSP booklet *Summary of the Thrift Savings Plan*. You may also want to use the resources available in the Planning & Tools section of the TSP website.

Your First Contribution

Your first contribution establishes your TSP account. If you were automatically enrolled, your contributions are made to the traditional balance of your TSP account until you make a different contribution election. Your contributions will automatically be invested in the Government Securities Investment (G) Fund until you make a different choice. See "Investing in the TSP" on page 12, which describes your TSP investment options and the actions you need to take to select them.

Starting or Changing Your Contributions

You can start, change, or stop any of your regular employee contributions at any time by submitting the TSP Election Form (TSP-1 for civilians; TSP-U-1 for members of the uniformed services) to your agency or service, or using your agency's or service's electronic version of the form. If you would like to start, stop, or change your catch-up contributions, submit Form TSP-1-C, Catch-Up Contribution Election (TSP-U-1-C for members of the uniformed services) to your agency or service.

Internal Revenue Code (IRC) Contribution Limits

The IRC places a number of specific limits on the dollar amount that you (and your employing agency on your behalf) can contribute to employer-sponsored plans like the TSP each year. These limits can change annually. When the annual limits become available, the TSP announces them on the TSP website and the ThriftLine, as well as through its various publications.

- The IRC elective deferral limit is an annual dollar limit, established under IRC section 402(g), that limits the amount of traditional and Roth employee contributions that a participant can make to employer-sponsored plans like the TSP. For 2014, the elective deferral limit is $17,500.

Note for FERS employees: If you reach the IRC elective deferral limit before the end of the year, your own contributions — and any associated Agency Matching Contributions — will be suspended. If you contribute to the TSP as a member of the Ready Reserve and as a civilian FERS participant, be sure that your combined contributions do not cause you to reach the IRC elective deferral limit before the end of the calendar year. If you do, you could lose out on matching contributions from your civilian agency. Use the calculator: How Much Can I Contribute? on the TSP website to avoid losing valuable agency matching money.

- The IRC annual additions limit is an annual dollar limit, established under IRC section 415(c), that limits the total amount of all contributions (traditional, Roth, tax-exempt, and all agency contributions) that can be made by a participant or on behalf of a participant to employer-sponsored plans like the TSP. For 2014, the section 415(c) limit is $52,000.

- The IRC catch-up contribution limit is an annual dollar limit, established under IRC section 414(v), that limits the amount of catch-up traditional and Roth employee contributions that a participant age 50 or older can make to employer-sponsored plans like the TSP. It is separate from the elective deferral limit and the annual additions limit. For 2014, the catch-up contribution limit is $5,500.

Note for members of the uniformed services: Contributions made from tax-exempt pay to a *traditional balance* do not count towards the elective deferral limit. These contributions are only subject to the annual additions limit. Contributions made from tax-exempt pay to a *Roth balance* count towards the elective deferral limit *and* the annual additions limit. If you also contribute to a civilian TSP account, total contributions to both accounts cannot exceed the IRC limits.

Account Security

Your TSP Account Number

Once your account has been established, the TSP will mail you a "welcome letter" containing your 13-digit account number and the identifying information your agency or service has provided to the TSP. This account number will be the TSP's primary means of identifying your account.

Web Password and ThriftLine PIN

Separately, you will receive a Web password for accessing your account on the TSP website. When you log into your account for the first time using this password, you will be prompted to change it to one of your choice. You will also receive a 4-digit Personal Identification Number (PIN), which you will need to access your account on the ThriftLine (1-TSP-YOU-FRST), the TSP's automated voice response system. You will need your account number and either a Web password or ThriftLine PIN to access your account through the website or ThriftLine, respectively.

You can change your Web password at any time through the My Account section of the TSP website. You can also change your ThriftLine PIN to one of your choice by accessing your account on the ThriftLine. Your change will take effect immediately.

Web User ID

Although you cannot change your TSP account number, you can create a customized Web user ID to log into your account through the TSP website. This user ID will not be valid for any other TSP purpose, but will help if you have difficulty remembering your 13-digit account number. You can establish a user ID by accessing your account on the TSP website.

Requesting an Account Number, Web Password, or ThriftLine PIN

If you forget your account number, you can use either the TSP website or ThriftLine to request that it be mailed to you again. If you lose your Web password, you can request a new one through the My Account section of the TSP website. If you lose your PIN, you can request a new one on the ThriftLine. You can also contact the TSP. If you make a written request, you must include your TSP account number and date of birth in your letter.

You should receive your remailed account number, new Web password, or new PIN within 10 days of the TSP receiving your request. In the meantime, you may not be able to access your account through the TSP website or ThriftLine.

Account Protection

Safeguard your TSP account number, Web password, ThriftLine PIN, and customized Web user ID to protect your account. The TSP is not responsible for losses resulting from the unauthorized use of your account number, Web password, ThriftLine PIN, or Web user ID. When using the TSP website, please ensure that your computer is protected against the latest viruses, Trojans, and keylogger software. Additional information about Internet security is available in the Security Center section of the TSP website and on many government websites such as www.consumer.gov/idtheft or www.OnGuardOnline.gov. The TSP is not responsible for losses resulting from the use of a compromised computer.

TSP Beneficiaries

Your Beneficiary Designation

You can designate one or more persons, a trust, or another entity to receive your TSP account in the event of your death. To designate beneficiaries, complete Form TSP-3, Designation of Beneficiary. The form is available on the TSP website or from your agency or service TSP representative.

If you make a valid beneficiary designation for your TSP account, you will receive a confirmation of your designation in the mail. Alternatively, if your designation is invalid and cannot be processed, you will be notified by the TSP.

If you do not designate beneficiaries, in the event of your death, your account will be distributed in accordance with the following order of precedence:

1. To your spouse;

2. If none, to your child or children equally, and descendants of deceased children by representation;

3. If none, to your parents equally or to the surviving parent;

4. If none, to the appointed executor or administrator of your estate; or

5. If none, to your next of kin who is entitled to your estate under the laws of the state in which you resided at the time of your death.

Be sure to keep your beneficiary designation up-to-date to reflect changes in your life, such as marriage, births, adoptions, divorce — even a change of address for your beneficiaries. Send a new Form TSP-3 to change a beneficiary designation or to update information.

A will is not a substitute for a Designation of Beneficiary form and will not be accepted for the distribution of your TSP account.

Beneficiary Participant Accounts

All death benefits of $200 or more that are processed for a spouse beneficiary are automatically deposited into a new TSP account established in the spouse's name. Beneficiary participants will be able to manage their investments and are eligible for the same withdrawal options as separated participants. Upon the death of a beneficiary participant, the account must be distributed to the new beneficiary(ies); it cannot remain in the TSP. For more information, see the booklet *Your TSP Account: A Guide for Beneficiary Participants*. You may also visit the Beneficiary Participants section of the TSP website.

Investing in the TSP

Whether you are automatically enrolled in the TSP, or you elect to participate in the TSP, your contributions will be initially invested in the Government Securities Investment (G) Fund until you make a different choice. The TSP offers you two approaches to investing your account:

- Lifecycle Funds (L Funds)

- Individual TSP Funds (G, F, C, S, and I Funds)

Lifecycle (L) Funds

The L Funds offer an easy option for those participants who do not have the time, interest, or knowledge to manage their TSP investments.

The L Funds are "lifecycle" funds that are invested according to a professionally determined mix of stocks, bonds, and securities based on various time horizons. (A time horizon is the date when you expect to withdraw your money.) L Funds with farther time horizons (for example, L 2050 and L 2040) are focused on growth, and therefore are invested more aggressively, with higher percentages in foreign and domestic stocks and lower percentages in Government securities. As each L Fund matures, its mix gradually shifts to more conservative investments with a higher percentage of Government securities and lower percentages of stocks. This more conservative mix is designed to preserve assets while still providing protection against inflation. (Detailed information about each L Fund is available on the TSP website.)

Each L Fund is automatically rebalanced, generally each business day, to restore the fund to its intended investment mix. Each quarter, the fund's asset allocation is adjusted to slightly more conservative investments. When an L Fund reaches its time horizon, it will roll into the L Income Fund, and a new fund will be added with a more distant time horizon.

The TSP offers five L Funds based on time horizon:

* L 2050 — 2045 and later

* L 2040 — 2035 through 2044

* L 2030 — 2025 through 2034

* L 2020 — 2015 through 2024

* L Income — Now withdrawing or expect to begin withdrawing before 2015

If you decide to invest your entire account in one of the L Funds, you are done making your investment decisions. Your L Fund will automatically rebalance based on your time horizon.

Individual TSP Funds

The TSP has five individual investment funds:

Government Securities Investment (G) Fund — invested in short-term, U.S. Treasury securities that are specially issued to the TSP (Government securities with no risk of loss)

Fixed Income Index Investment (F) Fund — invested in a bond index fund that tracks the Barclays Capital U.S. Aggregate Bond Index (U.S.

investment-grade corporate, Government, and mortgage-backed securities)

Common Stock Index Investment (C) Fund — invested in a stock index fund that tracks the Standard & Poor's 500 (S&P 500) Stock Index (primarily large U.S. companies)

Small Capitalization Stock Index Investment (S) Fund — invested in a stock index fund that tracks the Dow Jones U.S. Completion Total Stock Market Index (medium to small U.S. companies)

International Stock Index Investment (I) Fund — invested in a stock index fund that tracks the Morgan Stanley Capital International EAFE (Europe, Australasia, Far East) Stock Index (primarily large companies in 22 developed countries)

Visit the TSP website for detailed fund descriptions and information on fund performance.

If you choose your own investment mix from the G, F, C, S, and I Funds, remember that your investment allocation is one of the most important factors affecting the growth of your TSP account. If you prefer this "hands-on" approach, keep the following points in mind:

- *Consider both risk and return.* Over a long period of time, the F Fund (bonds) and the C, S, and I Funds (stocks) have higher potential returns than the G Fund (Government securities). But stocks and bonds also carry the risk of investment losses, which the G Fund does not. On the other hand, investing entirely in the G Fund may not give you the returns you need to meet your retirement savings goal.

- *You need to be comfortable with the amount of risk you expect to take.* Your investment comfort zone should allow you to use a "buy and hold" strategy so that you are not chasing market returns during upswings, or abandoning your investment strategy during downswings.

14

- *You can reduce your overall risk by diversifying your account.* The five individual TSP funds offer a broad range of investment options, including Government securities, bonds, and domestic and foreign stocks. Generally, it's best not to put "all of your eggs in one basket."

- *The amount of risk you can sustain depends upon your investment time horizon.* The more time you have before you need to withdraw your account, the more risk you can take. (This is because early losses can be offset by later gains.)

- *Periodically review your investment choices.* Check the distribution of your account balance among the funds to make sure that the mix you chose is still appropriate for your situation. If not, rebalance your account to get the allocation you want.

Deciding on Your Approach

The TSP investment options are designed for you to choose *either* the L Fund that is appropriate for your time horizon *or* a combination of the individual TSP funds that will support your personal investment strategy. However, you are permitted to invest in any fund or combination of funds. Just keep in mind that the L Funds are made up of the five individual TSP funds (G, F, C, S, and I). If you invest in an L Fund as well as in the individual funds, you will duplicate some of your investments, and your allocation may not be what you wanted.

Implementing Your Investment Choice

Once you have decided on your investment approach — professionally designed (L Funds) or self-directed (individual TSP funds) — there are two transactions you can make to put your money in the fund(s) you have chosen:

- The first transaction you need to make is a *contribution allocation*. This transaction directs how new money (contributions, transfers into the TSP, loan payments) will be invested. It does not change your existing account balance.

- The second transaction you may want to make is an *interfund transfer (IFT)*. An IFT is a transaction that allows you to redistribute all or part of your existing TSP account among the different TSP funds. For each calendar month, your first two IFTs can redistribute money in your account among any or all of the TSP funds. After that, for the remainder of the month, your IFTs can only move money into the Government Securities Investment (G) Fund (in which case, you will increase the percentage of your account held in the G Fund by reducing the percentage held in one or more of the other TSP funds). An IFT has no effect on new money coming into your account. The transfer counts in the calendar month we process it, not in the month you submit it.

If you have a civilian and a uniformed services account, these transactions apply to each account separately.

If you have a traditional and a Roth balance, any contribution allocations or interfund transfers you make will apply to both balances. You cannot make a separate contribution allocation or interfund transfer for each balance.

You can perform these transactions in the My Account section of the TSP website, using your TSP account number (or customized Web user ID) and Web password, or you can request these transactions through the ThriftLine, using your TSP account number and PIN.

Transferring Other Investments Into Your TSP Account

If your TSP account has already been established and you have a balance, you can transfer money from your traditional IRA or eligible employer plan into your TSP account. This money will be invested according to your most recent contribution allocation. To transfer tax-deferred money into the traditional balance of your TSP account, use Form TSP-60, Request for a Transfer into the TSP. To transfer Roth money into the Roth balance of your TSP account, use Form TSP-60-R, Request for a Roth Transfer into the TSP. Both forms are available on the TSP website. Note: You cannot transfer any money from a Roth IRA into your TSP account.

Account Information

Your Account Balance

Your account balance (expressed in both dollars and shares) is available in the My Account section of the TSP website and on the ThriftLine. Your account balance is updated at the end of each business day based on that day's closing share prices and any transactions processed that night.

Your Participant Statements

Your first quarterly statement will be mailed to you. After that, quarterly statements will be available only on the TSP website unless you make a request to continue receiving them in the mail. You can make this request on the TSP website or the ThriftLine.

You will also receive an annual participant statement at the beginning of each calendar year. That statement will provide a summary of your account activity for the previous year and give you other information, such as an account profile and your cumulative lifetime contributions to the TSP. You should review and verify all the information on this statement.

Check all your statements to ensure that:

- your personal information (name, address, date of birth, etc.) is correct;

- the contribution amount is correct;

- payments on any loans you may have are being deposited correctly; and

- transactions (interfund transfers, loans, withdrawals, etc.) have been properly recorded.

Correcting Your Account Information

To correct personal information (e.g., address, date of birth, etc.), active employees and members of the uniformed services must have their agencies or services make any corrections to their TSP account records. Separated participants must notify the TSP directly. Separated participants can also make address changes on the TSP website or send Form TSP-9, Change in Address for Separated Participant, to the TSP.

To update your beneficiary information or to change your beneficiary(ies), send a new Form TSP-3, Designation of Beneficiary, directly to the TSP.

If you change agencies (or payroll offices), make sure that your TSP contributions (and your loan payments, if any) continue after you transfer. Report any errors to your new payroll office immediately, and follow up to make sure the corrections took effect.

Getting Your Money Out[6]

Automatic Enrollment Refunds

Generally, if you were automatically enrolled in the TSP, you have 90 days from the date of your first contribution to request a refund of your own automatic enrollment contributions and earnings using Form TSP-25, Automatic Enrollment Refund Request. If you are a FERS employee, you will forfeit your Agency Matching Contributions, but Agency Automatic (1%) Contributions will remain in your account.

Loans

The TSP loan program allows active eligible participants to borrow from their accounts and repay the loan with interest.

There are two types of loans:

- *General purpose loans,* which can be used for any purpose, have a repayment period of 1 to 5 years.

- *Residential loans,* which are available only for the purchase or construction of a primary residence, have a repayment period of 1 to 15 years.

To learn more about the loan program, you may visit the Loans and Withdrawals section of the TSP website, or read the TSP booklet *Loans,* which is available from the TSP website or from your agency or service. In particular, read the section that discusses the things to consider before you borrow; it will help you

---

[6] All loans and withdrawals are disbursed proportionally from any traditional and Roth balances in your account. Similarly, if you are a uniformed services member with tax-exempt contributions in your traditional balance, loans and withdrawals from your uniformed services account will contain a proportional amount of tax-exempt contributions as well. You cannot designate the type of money (traditional, Roth, or tax-exempt) that you want to borrow or withdraw.

decide whether your TSP account is your best option for borrowing money. Taking a loan can reduce your TSP balance at retirement because the interest rate you pay to your account for the loan may be less than the earnings you would have received if the money had remained in your account.

In-Service Withdrawals

If you are still employed by the Federal Government, you can withdraw money from your account only under the following circumstances:

- If you are age 59½ or older, you may make a one-time *age-based in-service withdrawal*.

  Note: When you make an age-based withdrawal, you lose the option of making a partial withdrawal from your account after you separate from service.

- If you have a financial hardship, you may make a *financial hardship in-service withdrawal* (limited to one every 6 months). You will not be allowed to make contributions to your account for 6 months after you make the withdrawal. (If you are a FERS employee, you will not receive Agency Matching Contributions during that time; Agency Automatic (1%) Contributions will continue.) In addition, if you are under age 59½, you may be required to pay an early withdrawal penalty tax.

Other restrictions apply to these withdrawals. For more information, visit the In-Service Withdrawals section of the TSP website. You should also read the TSP booklet *In-Service Withdrawals* and the TSP tax notice "Important Tax Information About Payments From Your TSP Account."

Post-Separation Withdrawals

When you leave Federal service, you have a number of withdrawal options:

- *Leave your money in the TSP*. If you have $200 or more, you can leave your account in the TSP. (If your vested account balance is less than $200, the TSP will automatically send you the entire amount in a single payment. You cannot leave it in the TSP.)

You must withdraw your account (or begin receiving monthly payments) by April 1 of the year following the year you turn 70½ and are no longer in Federal service.

If you have both a civilian and a uniformed services TSP account and you separate from Federal civilian service or from the uniformed services (or both), you may combine your TSP accounts. Use Form TSP-65, Request to Combine Civilian and Uniformed Services TSP Accounts.

- *Make a partial withdrawal.* You may make a one-time, single-payment, partial withdrawal (but only if you had not previously made an age-based in-service withdrawal).

- *Make a full withdrawal.* You have three options to withdraw your entire TSP account balance:

  - A single payment
  - TSP monthly payments
  - An annuity (purchased for you from the TSP's annuity vendor at a minimum of $3,500)[7]

  You can combine any of these three full withdrawal options.

You can also have the TSP transfer part or all of certain types of withdrawals to a traditional IRA, an eligible employer plan, or a Roth IRA.

When considering your withdrawal options, use the calculators on the TSP website to estimate the amount of annuity payments or monthly payments you might receive.

---

[7] If you have both a traditional and a Roth balance in your TSP account, the $3,500 minimum amount will apply to both balances separately. You cannot select just one balance for your annuity purchase, and you cannot select more than one type of annuity.

You can find more information about post-separation withdrawals by visiting the Withdrawals After Leaving Federal Service section of the TSP website. The booklet *Withdrawing Your TSP Account After Leaving Federal Service* also describes your TSP withdrawal options. In addition, you should read the TSP tax notice "Important Tax Information About Payments From Your TSP Account." The booklet and tax notice are available from the TSP website, your agency or service, or the TSP.

Spouses' Rights

Spouses' rights requirements apply to loans, in-service withdrawals, and post-separation withdrawals.

Loans, In-Service Withdrawals, and Partial Withdrawals. If you are a married FERS participant or a member of the uniformed services, your spouse must give written consent to your loan, or notarized written consent to your in-service or partial withdrawal request. If you are a married CSRS participant, the TSP will notify your spouse of your loan application or your partial or in-service withdrawal request.

Post-Separation Full Withdrawals. Spouses' rights requirements apply to vested accounts of more than $3,500. If you are a married FERS participant or a member of the uniformed services, your spouse is entitled to a prescribed joint life and survivor annuity. If you select any other withdrawal option (including any other annuity option), your spouse must first waive his or her right to the prescribed annuity. If you are a married CSRS participant, the TSP must notify your spouse of any withdrawal election.

Under certain limited circumstances, exceptions to these requirements may be granted. See Form TSP-16, Exception to Spousal Requirements (TSP-U-16 for members of the uniformed services), available on the TSP website.

Checklist for
New Participants

✓ If you are a new FERS participant, consider increasing your employee contributions to at least 5% of your basic pay to make sure that you earn the maximum agency matching funds.

✓ Safeguard your TSP account number, your Web password, your ThriftLine Personal Identification Number (PIN), and, if applicable, your customized Web user ID to protect your account.

✓ Investigate whether you want to make traditional (pre-tax) contributions, Roth (after-tax) contributions, or a combination of both.

✓ Read about your TSP investment options.

✓ Decide whether you want to use one of the TSP's professionally designed Lifecycle Funds or manage your own TSP investments.

✓ Make a *contribution allocation* to direct the way your future contributions are invested.

✓ Make an *interfund transfer* to move your existing account balance into the funds of your choice. (New accounts are invested in the G Fund.)

✓ Decide whether you want to designate beneficiaries for your account.

To learn more about the TSP, ask your agency or service for a copy of the *Summary of the Thrift Savings Plan*, or download one from the TSP website. The forms and publications referred to in this booklet can be obtained from the TSP website or your TSP representative.